DRAGONFLY COLORING BOOK

CRYSTAL
COLORING BOOKS

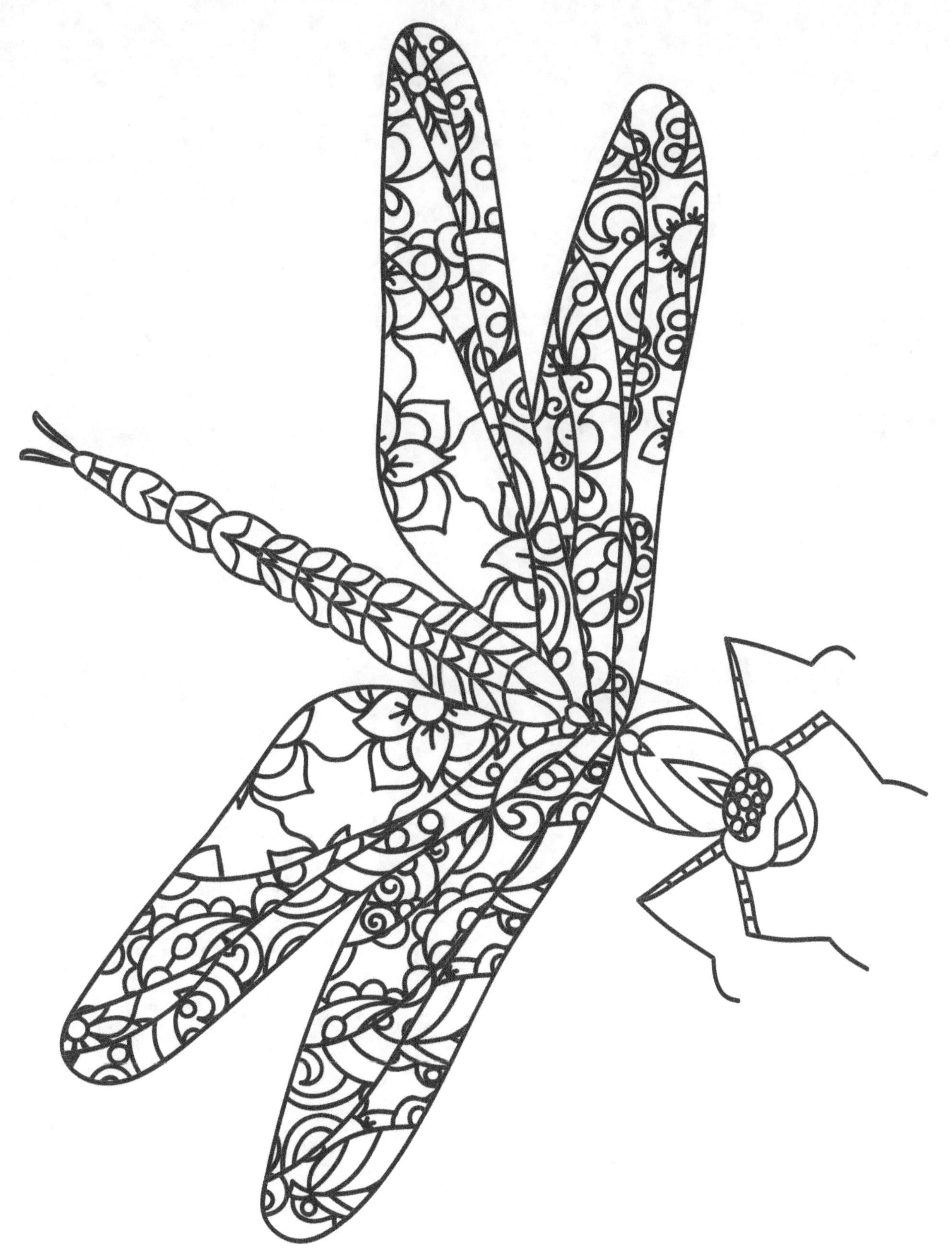

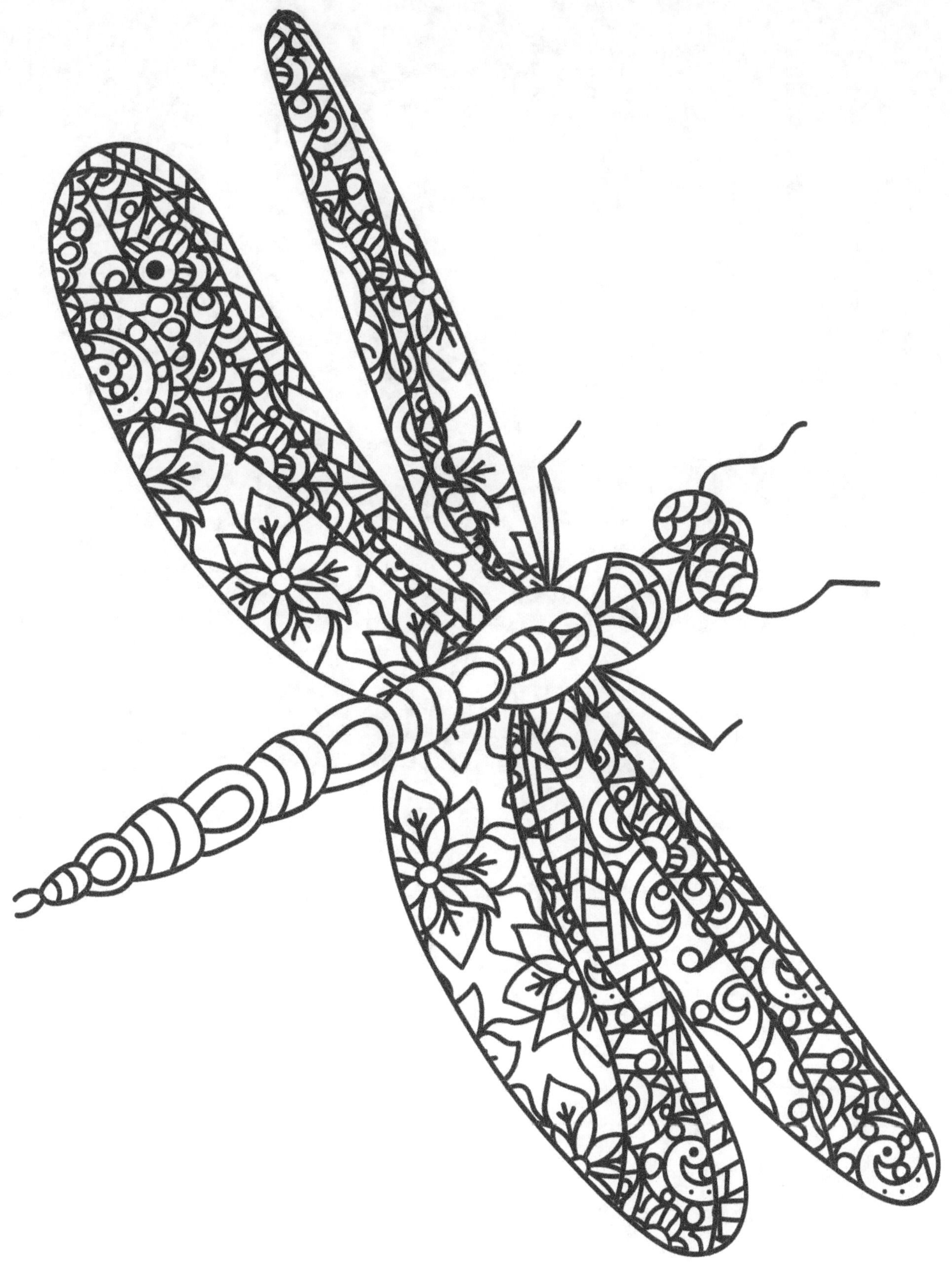

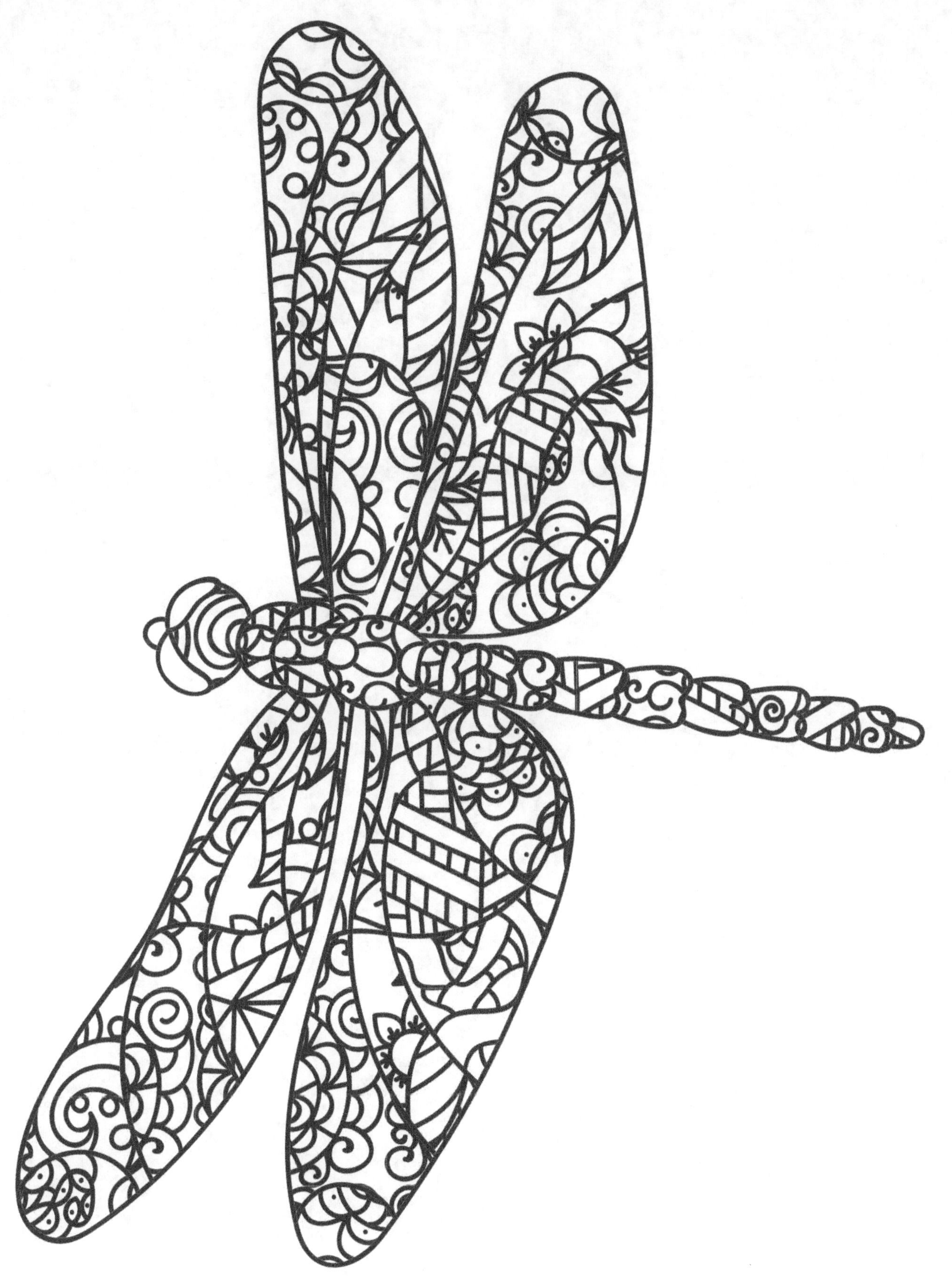

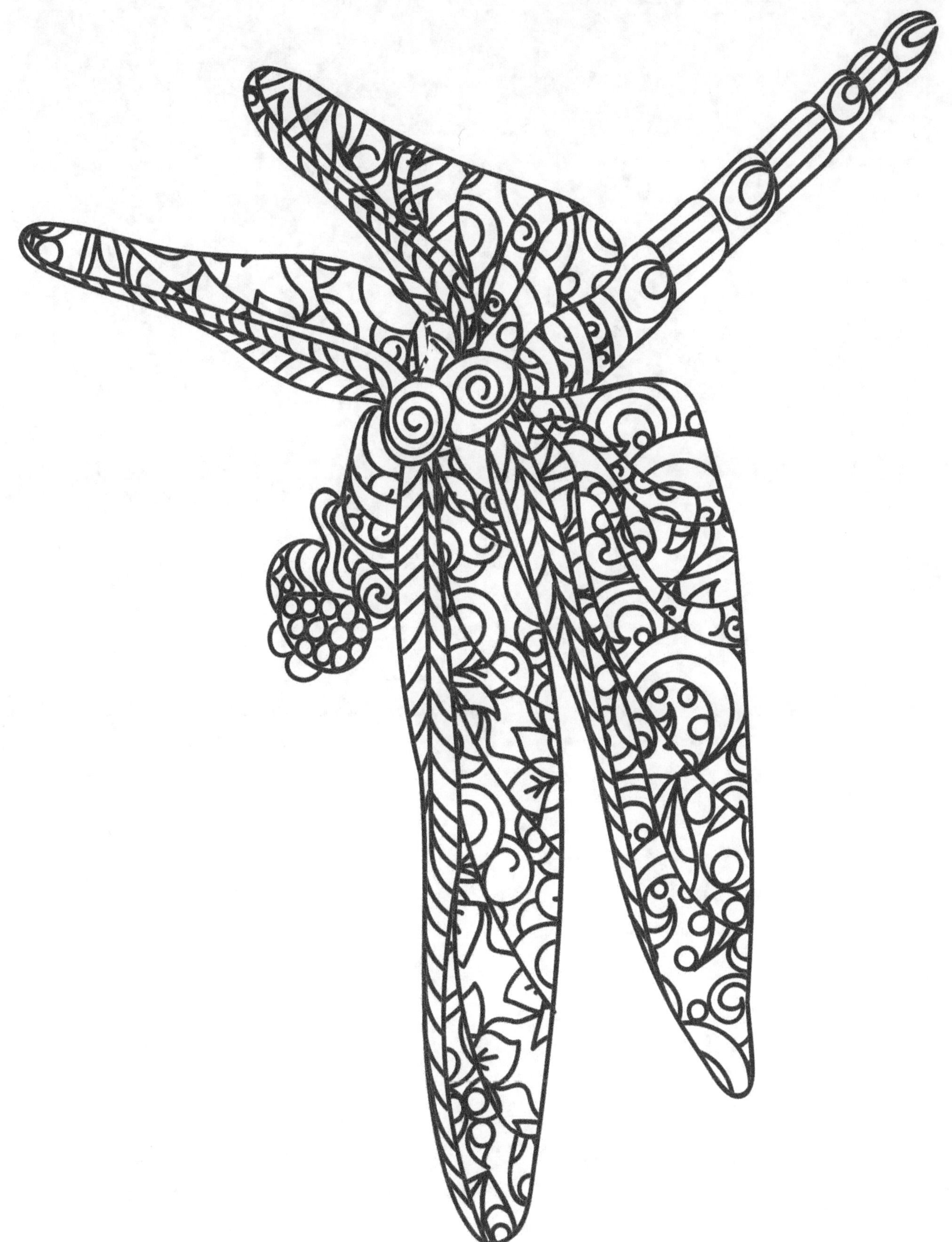

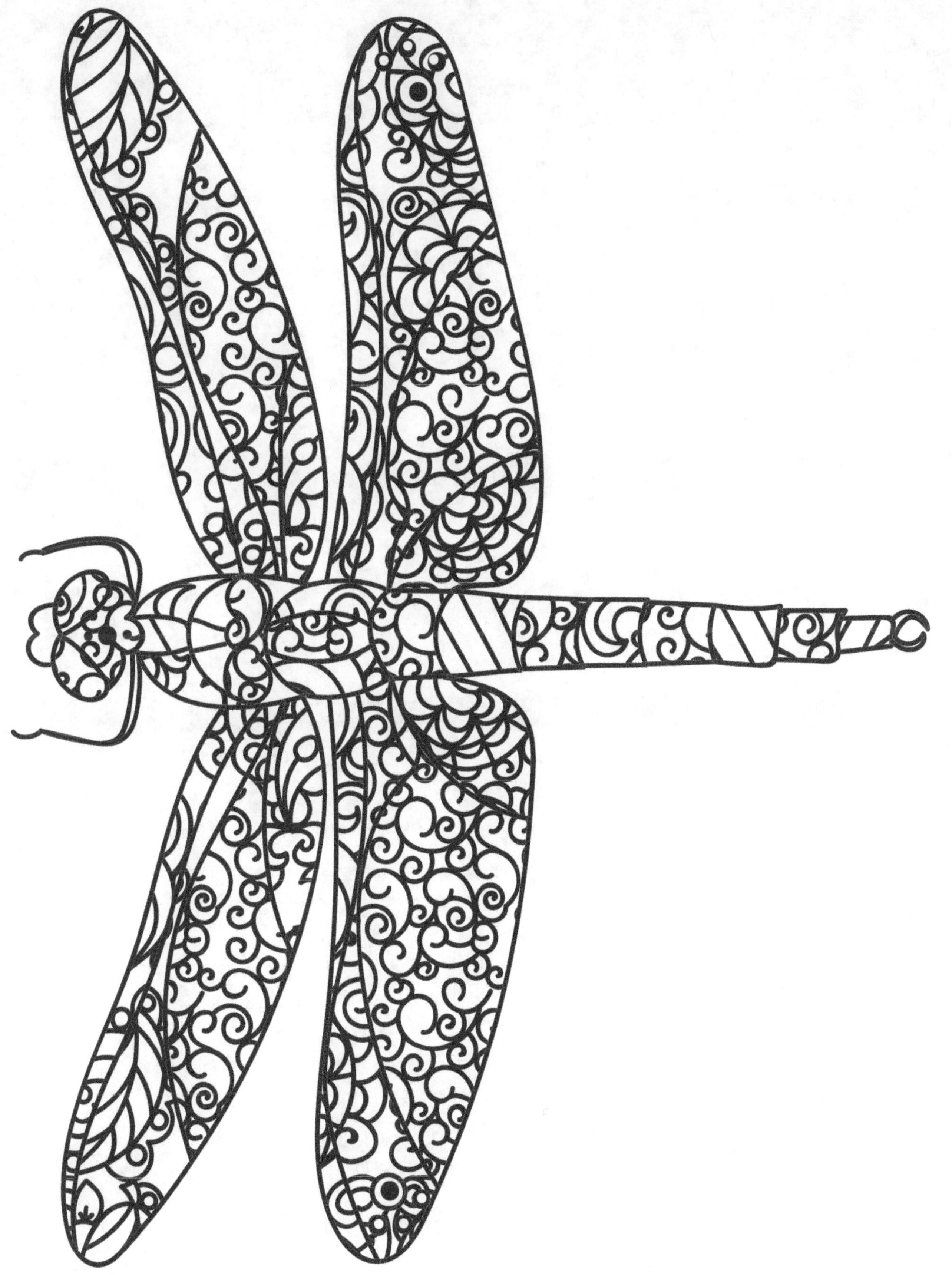

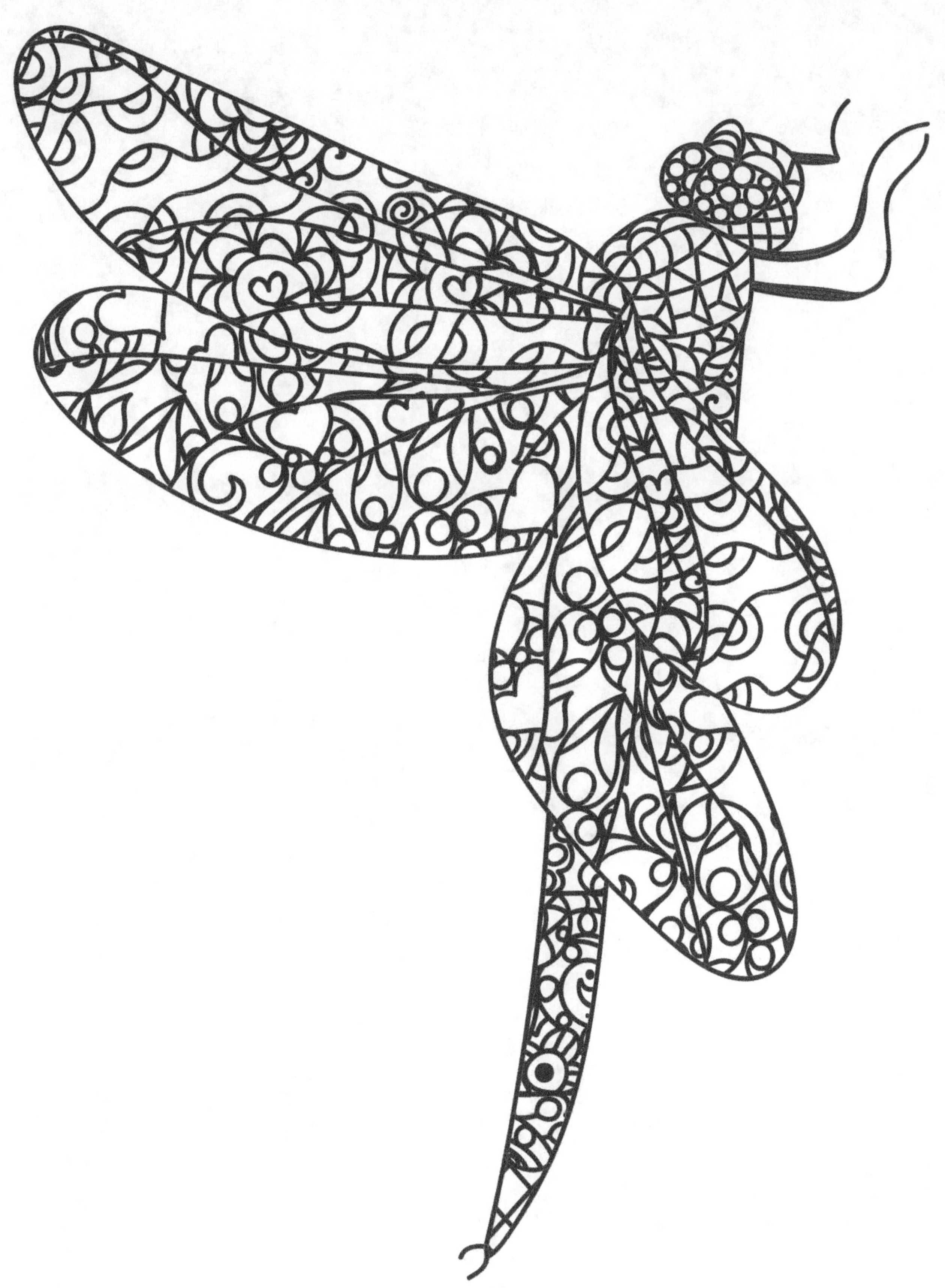

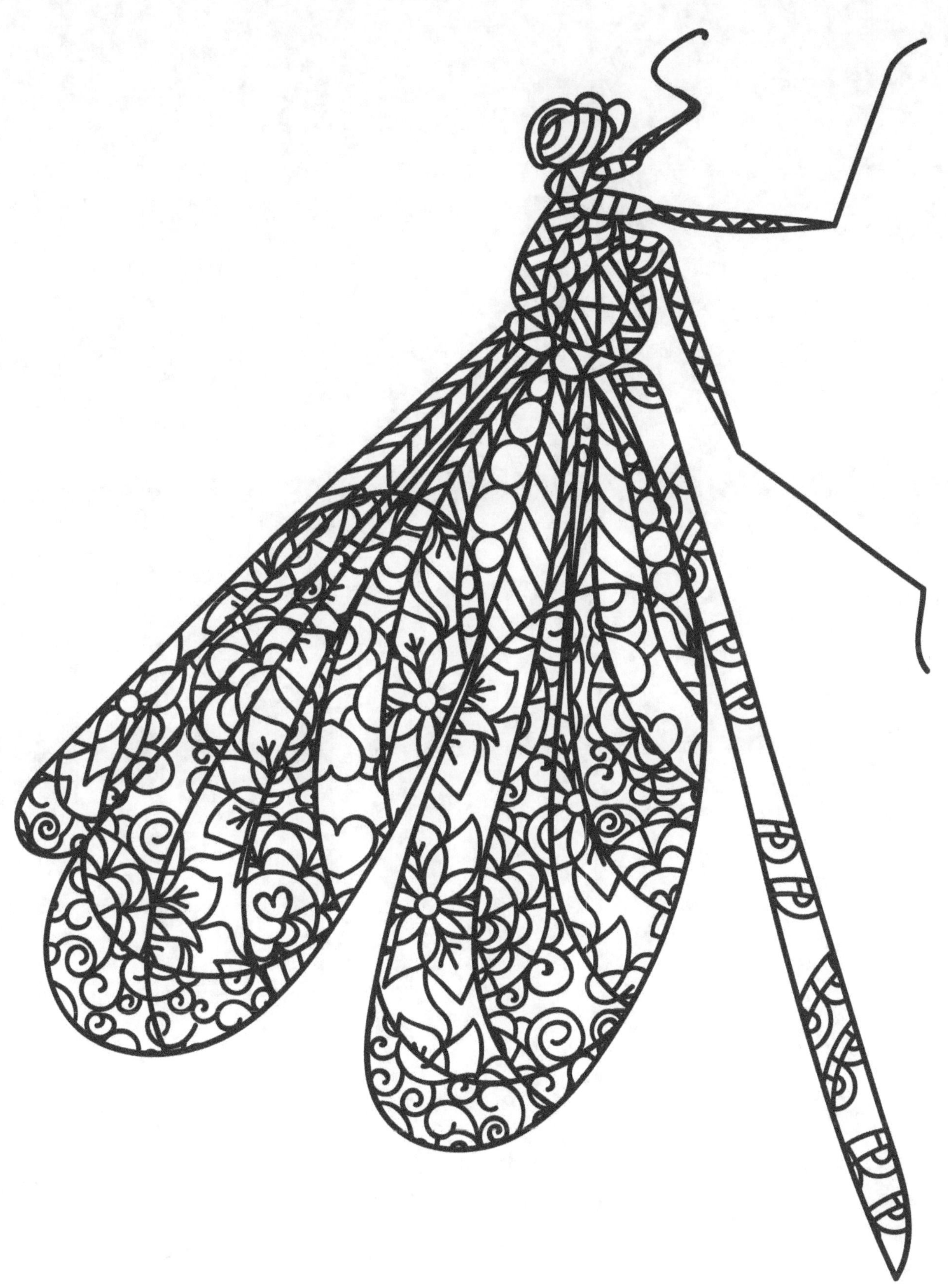

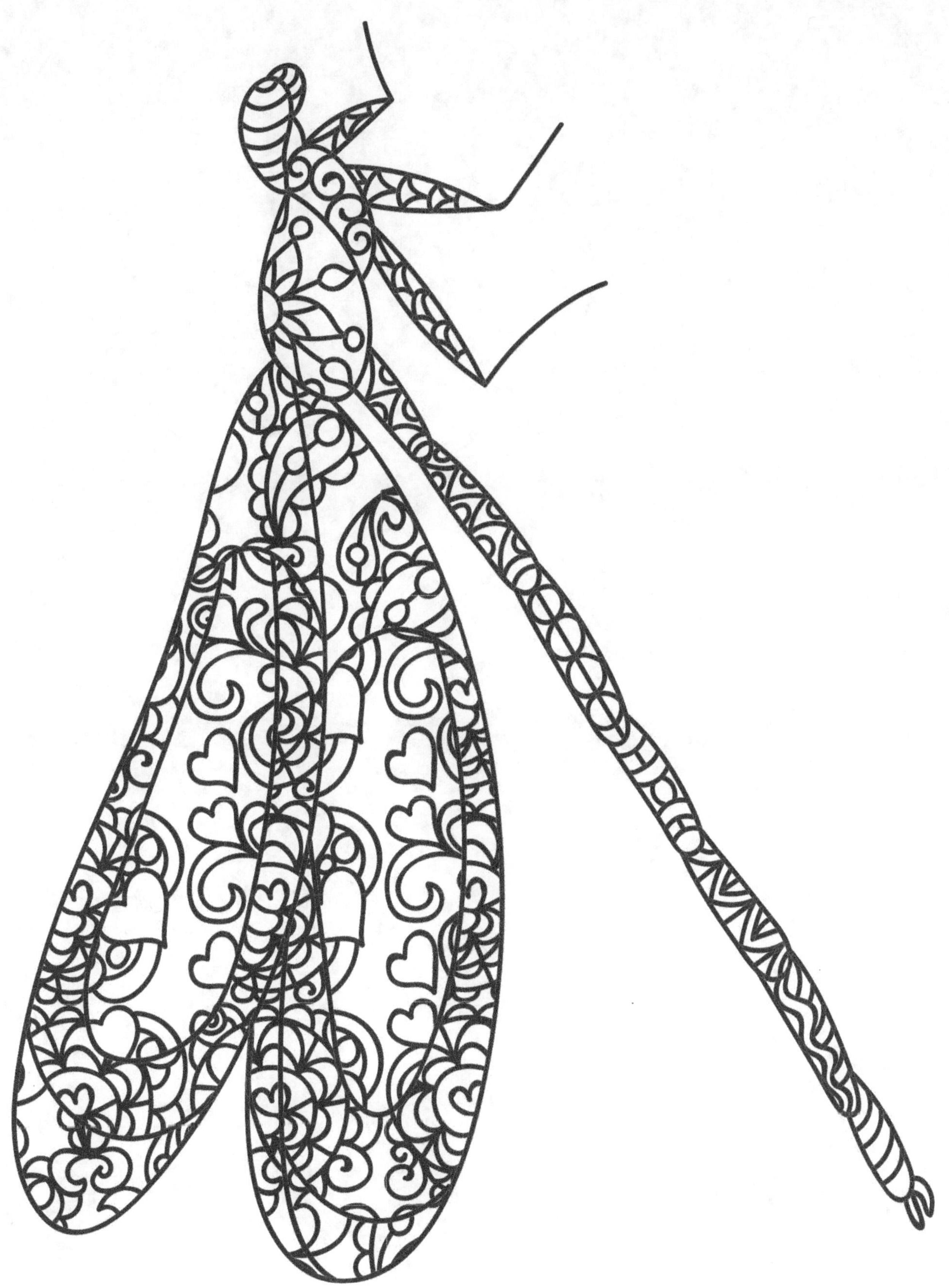

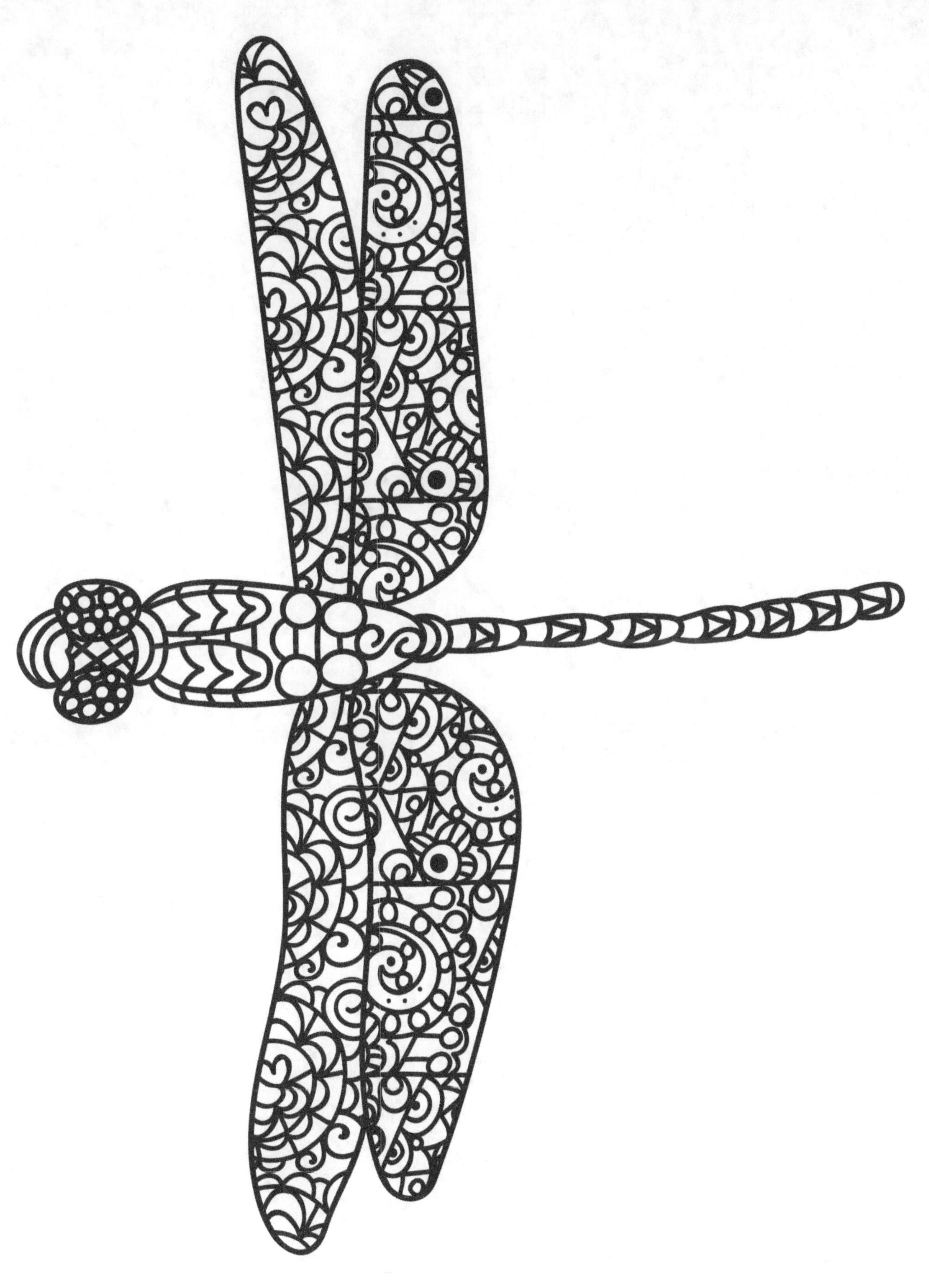

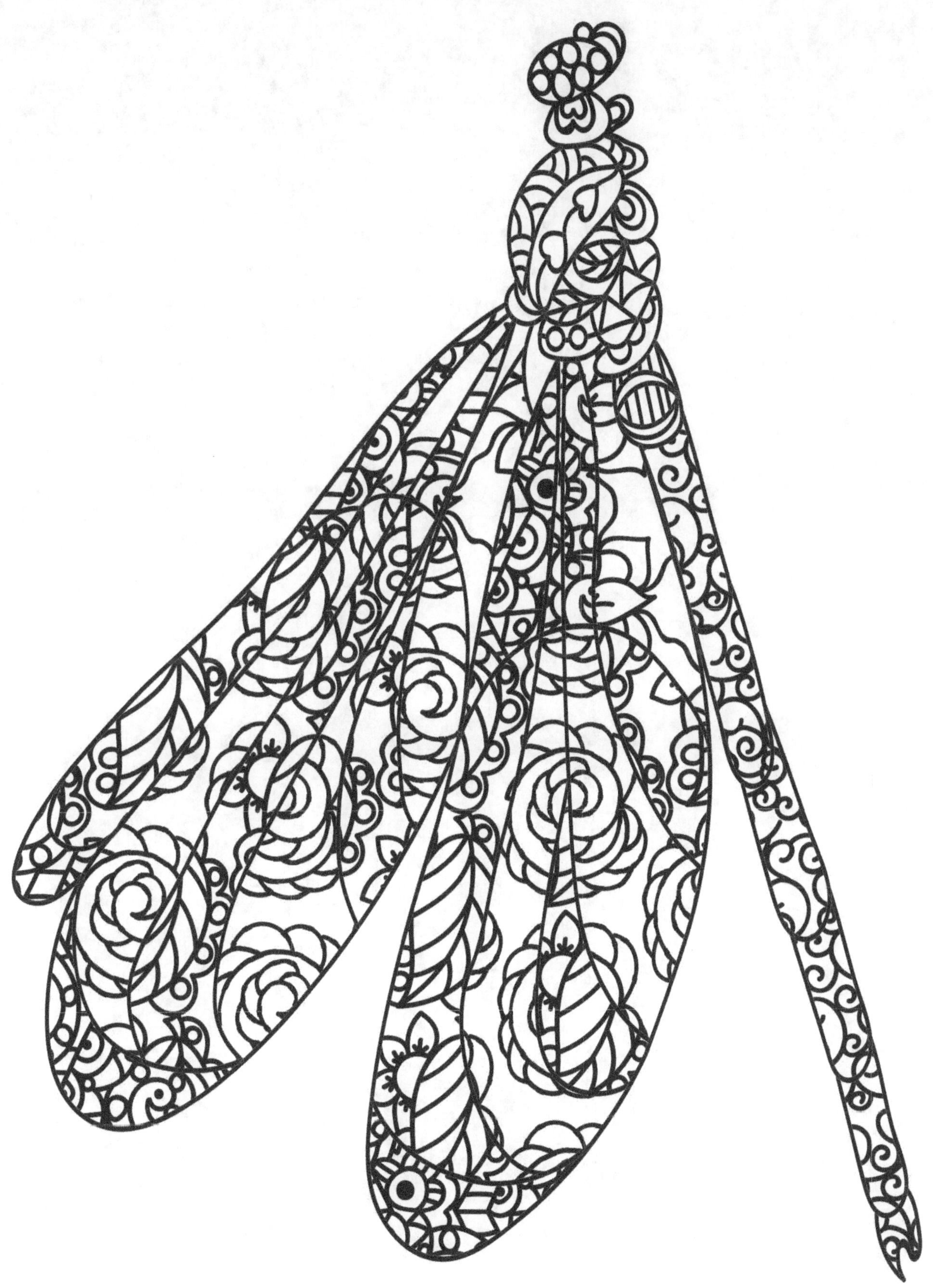

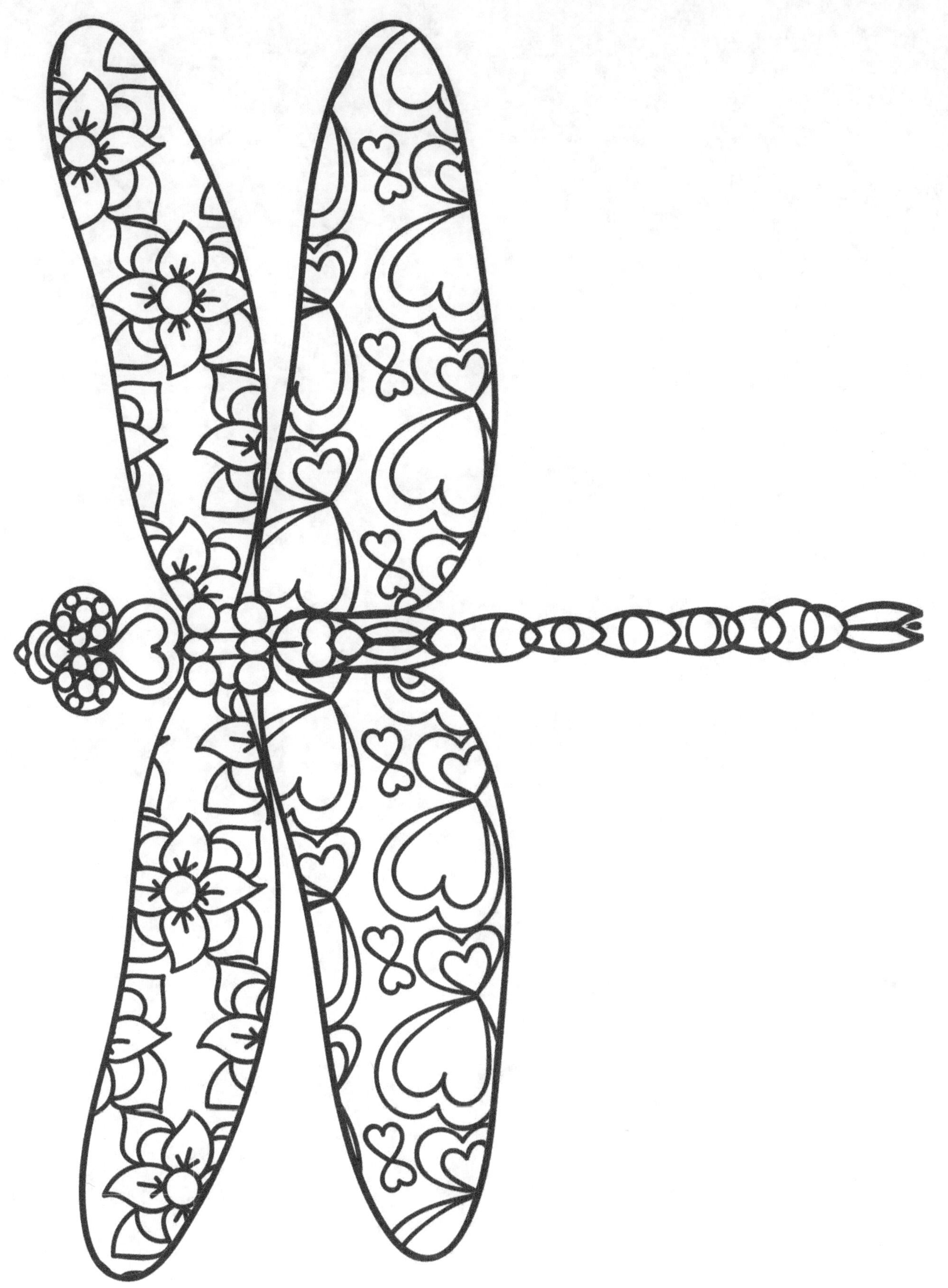

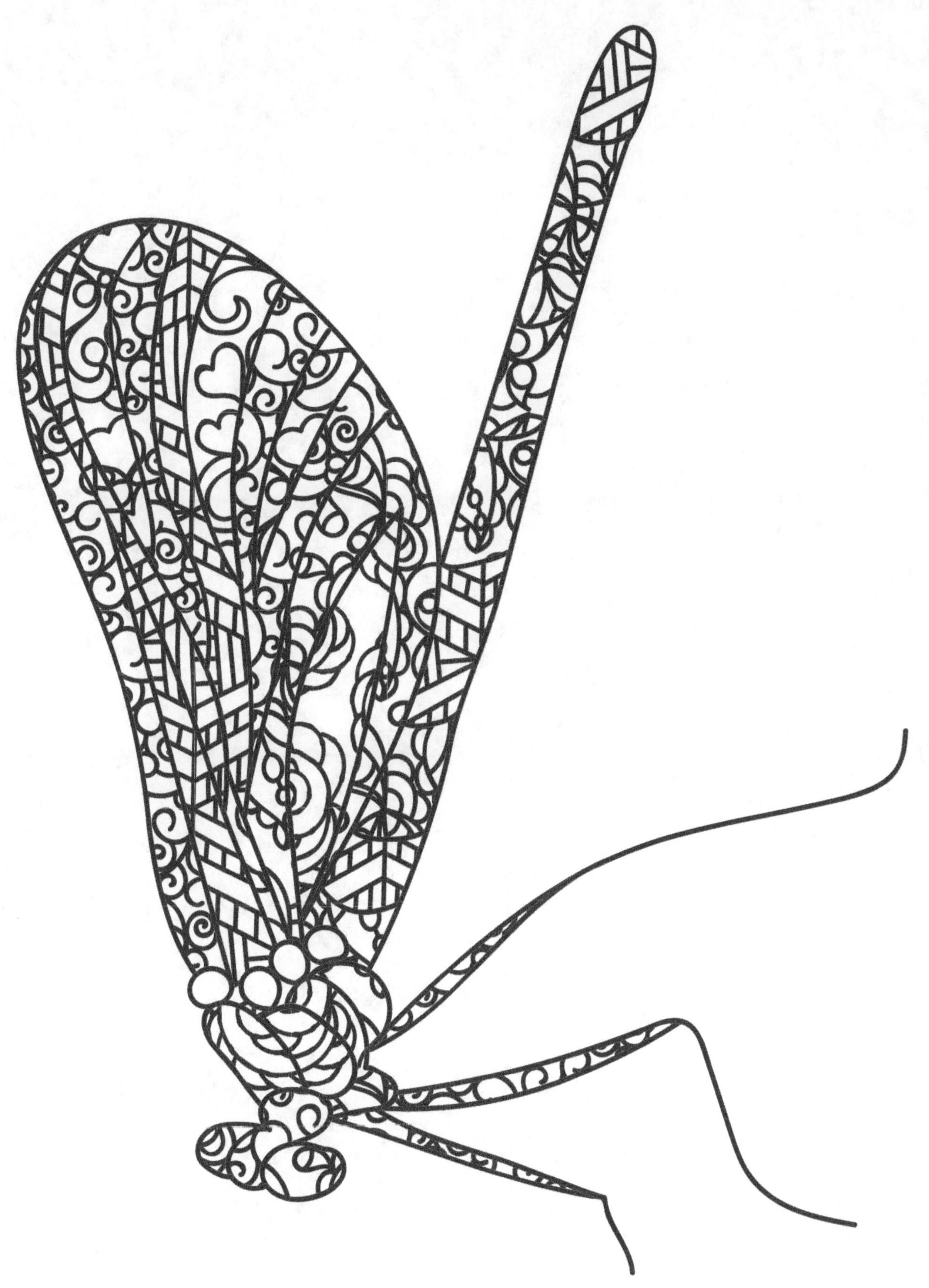

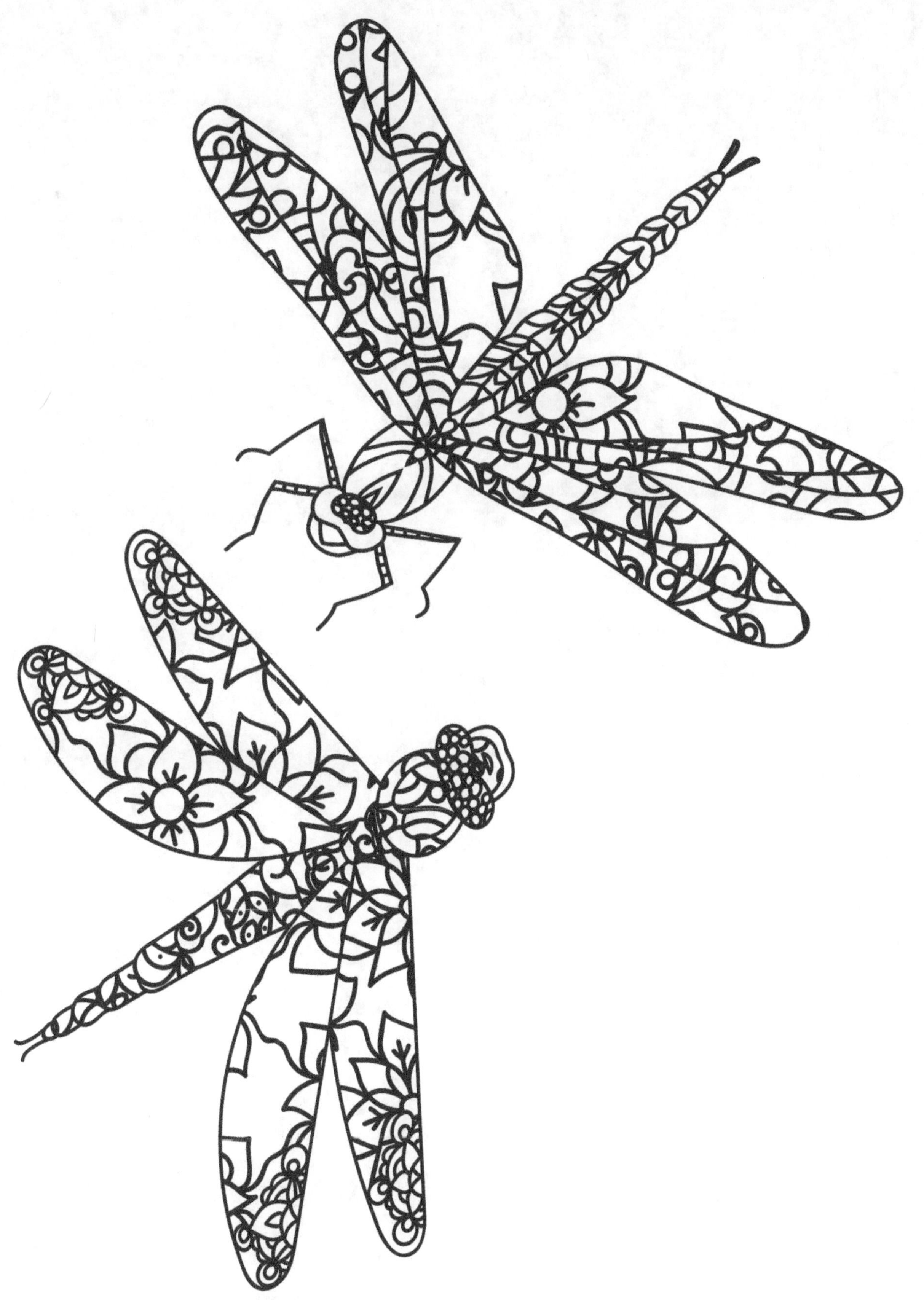

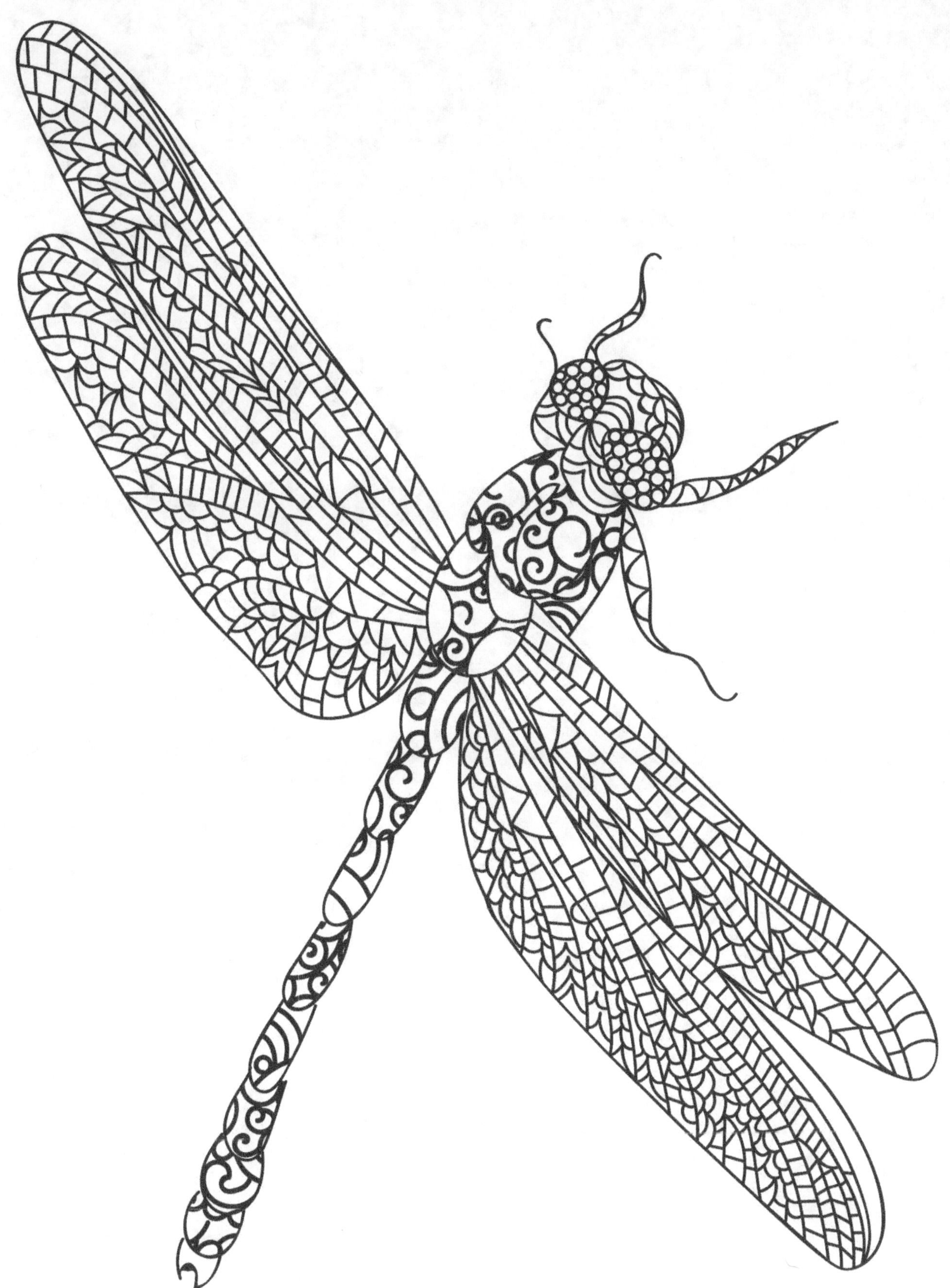

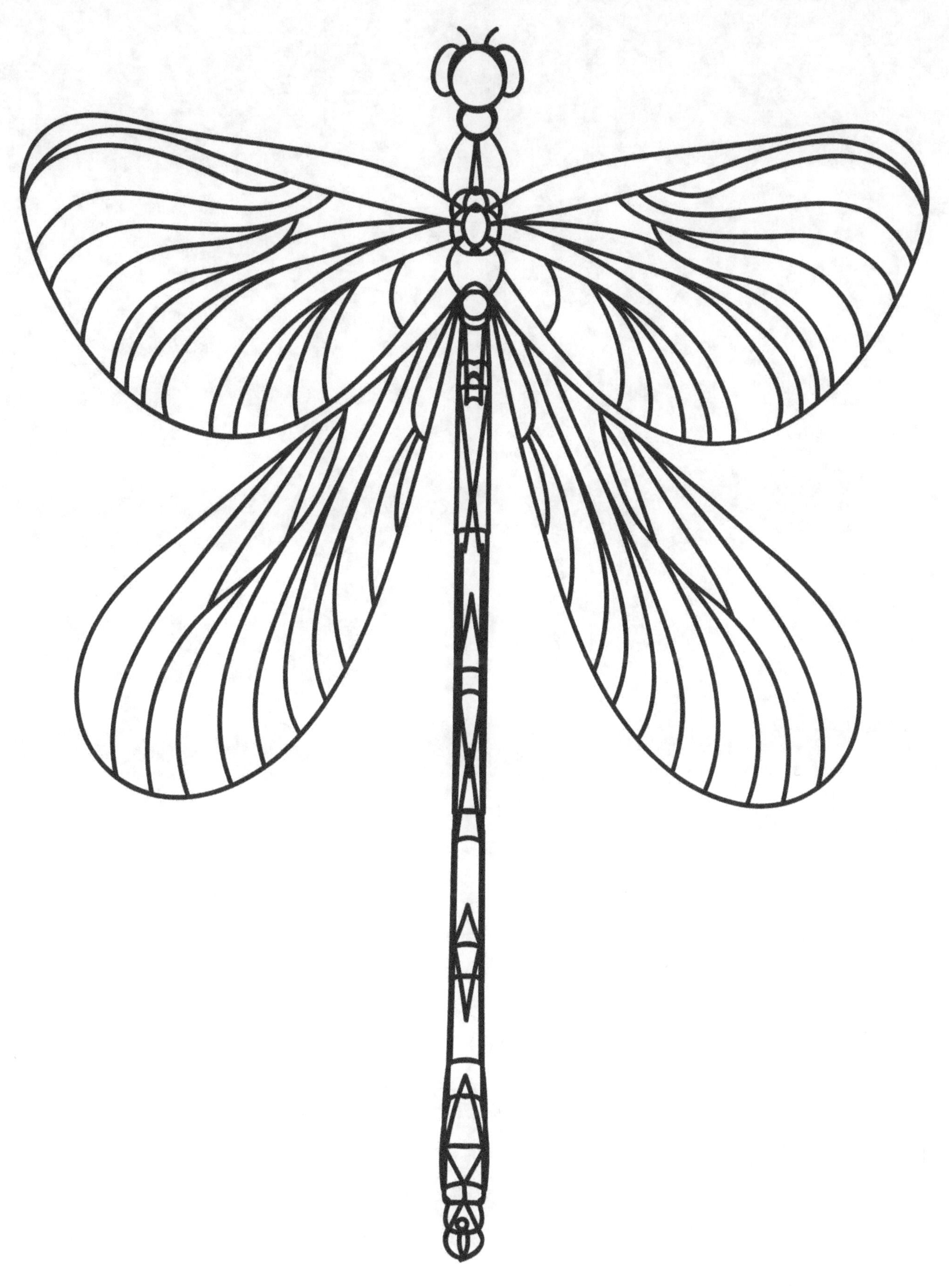

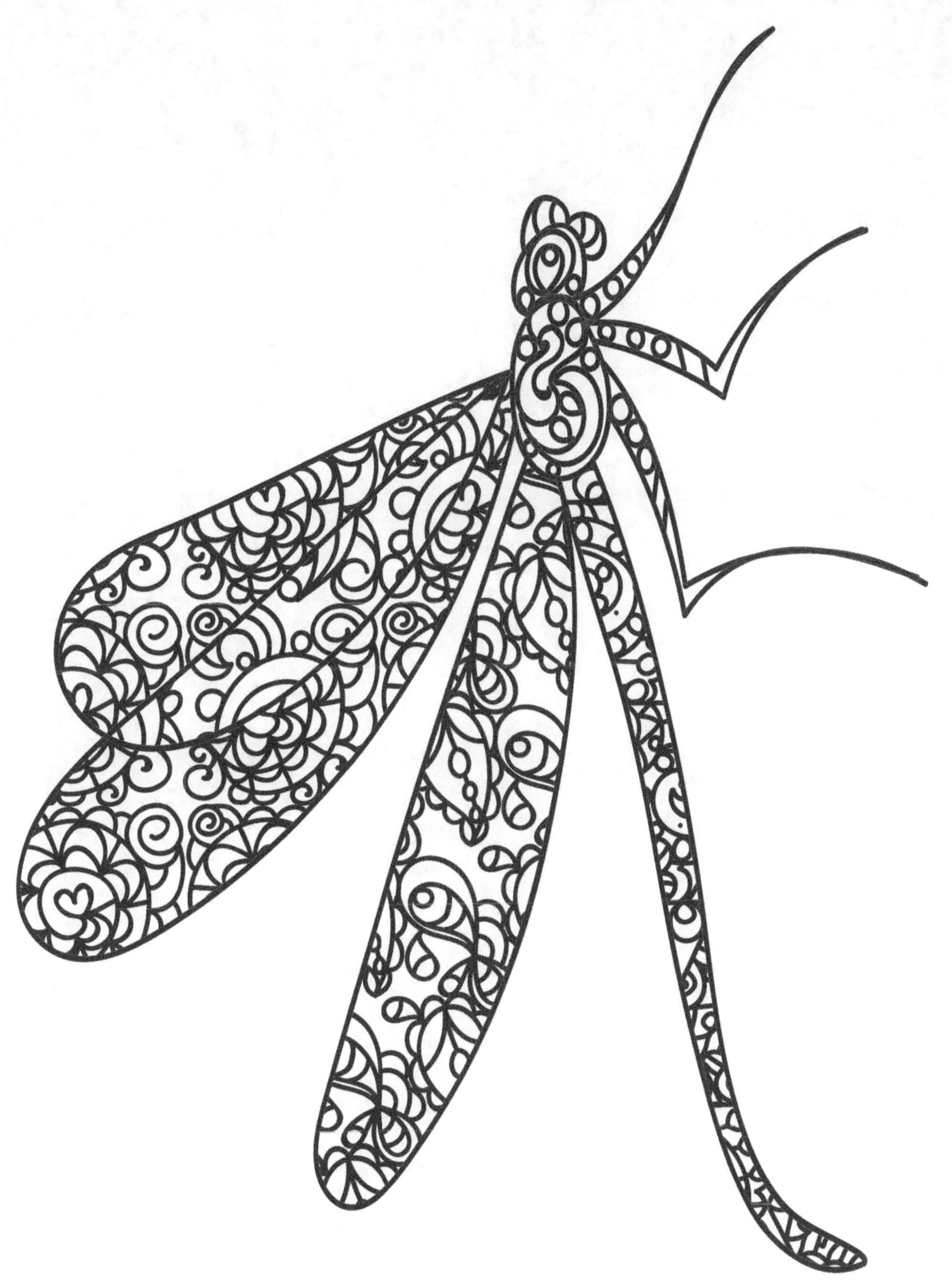

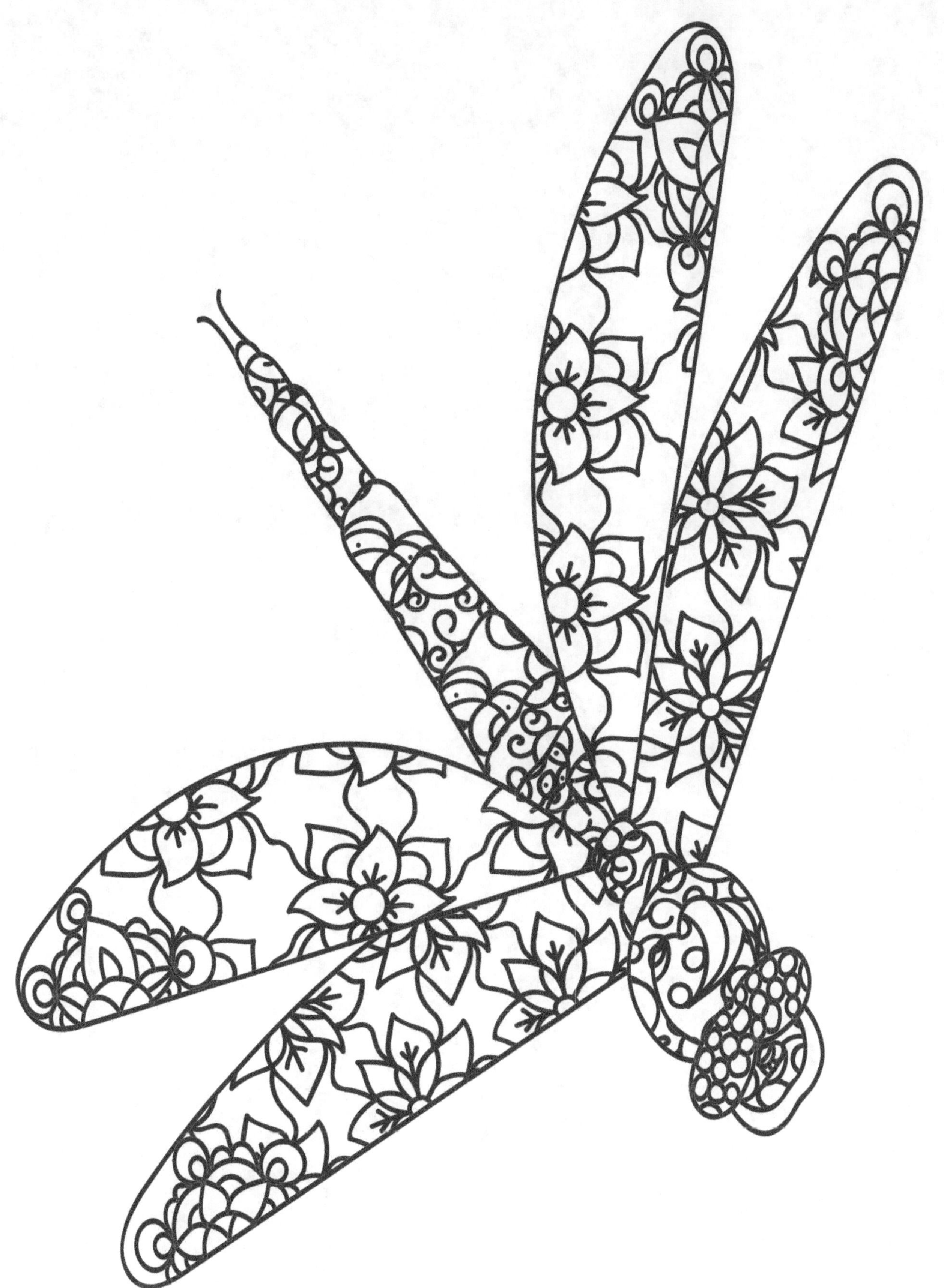

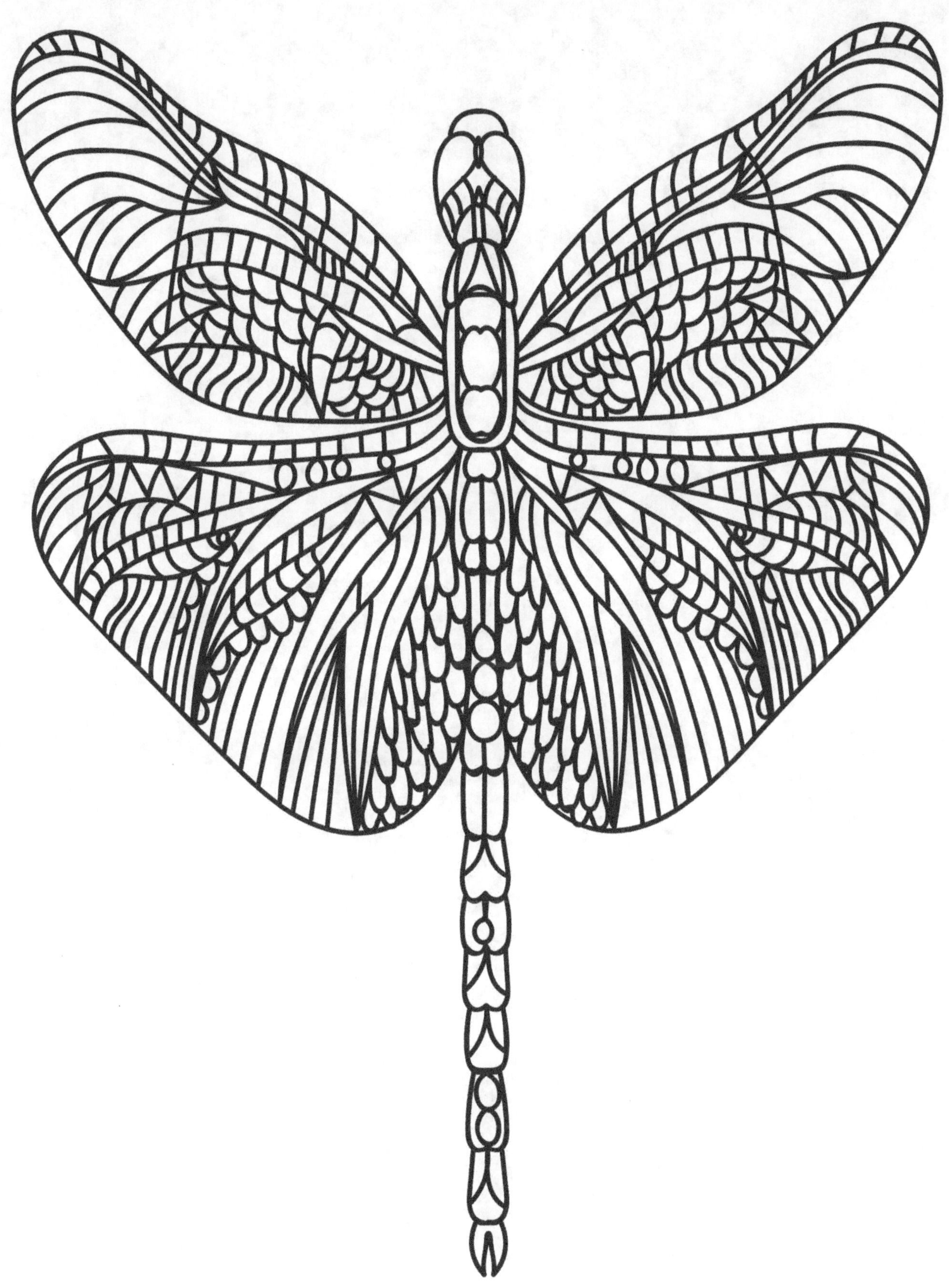

COLOR TEST PAGE

COLOR TEST PAGE

www.ingramcontent.com/pod-product-compliance
Lightning Source LLC
Chambersburg PA
CBHW080903260726
48660CB00009B/3424